T0137597

A Life's Tapestry

Donna J. Mertz – Author & Photographer

Order this book online at www.trafford.com
or email orders@trafford.com

Most Trafford titles are also available at major online book retailers.

Printed in Victoria, BC, Canada.

ISBN: 978-1-4269-3433-9

*Our mission is to efficiently provide the world's finest, most comprehensive book publishing
service, enabling every author to experience success. To find out how to publish your book, your
way, and have it available worldwide, visit us online at www.trafford.com*

Trafford rev. 6/8/2010

 www.trafford.com

North America & international
toll-free: 1 888 232 4444 (USA & Canada)
phone: 250 383 6864 ♦ fax: 812 355 4082

This book is dedicated to everyone who has touched my life with laughter, friendship, and love...making my life's tapestry beautiful and unique!

A Life's Tapestry

This collection of writings and photographs is meant to inspire, teach, motivate, & sometimes just to evoke a laugh.

Each turn of the page is a life lesson. Learned through experiences, strangers, friends, or loves along my life's journey.

Believing that everything happens for a reason: be it small or great: each life lesson is, in itself, important. As each thread in a tapestry does its part in keeping the whole tapestry together.

I believe that the beauty of these lessons, are meant to be shared so that others can begin to recognize the life lessons they have lived, and with their own threads, weave together a tapestry of their own that will create the balance of heart, mind, body, and soul necessary for a peaceful journey through the rest of this life.

Hoping to make you stop in your everyday for a moment, to show you the beauty in small things. Hoping to comfort you in your troubles and reassure you that you are not alone. Hoping to convince you that you are loved unconditionally and that He is always and forever helping you through this thing we call life. Hoping that by being here I can share with you the laughter that is essential for a happy heart, and to share with you small pieces of the beauty He has created

The proverbial (& literal) empty nest:
As much as it broke her heart, she nudged them over
the edge of the nest. Knowing that she had given them
all the love and care they needed to spread their wings,
and fly their own course…even so, they waited a while in
the rain to see if, maybe, she would call them back.
(With her heart aching so profoundly, she almost did)

Don't wait for me if you are ready to move on - you need to go ahead, I will follow if it is where my life is to go - if not - please smile at the memory of the people we were together and know that I am smiling too. We were good for each other, together we made it through some otherwise lonely times…because of that you will always be a part of me, and always be a fond memory, saved to look back on when days aren't so sunny and I need a smile.

As they settled down for an afternoon nap, in a
voice as gentle as a soft spring rain, she spoke:
"By balancing your heart, body, mind, & spirit, you will
become all that you can be & still grow to be more than
you dared to dream. Enjoy each other as long as you can
and rest assured that you are unconditionally loved."

As they drifted off to sleep, God smiled, hearing their unspoken
prayers…each giving thanks for the others. Proud as a Father
could be His gentle hands held them safely as they slept.

Riding elephants, chasing unicorns, watching the world spin
by in streaks of color, happy faces blurring and becoming one
big smile. Steal a taste of spun sugar; let it melt in your mouth
making your taste buds jump up and down and sing a happy
song of sweetness. Or just pick up a brush & paint with every
color of the rainbow, swirling them all together, paint a picture
of what happy looks like when you close your eyes…always let a
little paint get outside of the lines, always allow yourself to live a
little outside the lines, try something new, re-try something old…
never completely let go of your childhood dreams and fantasies.
Promise yourself that you will laugh whole-heartedly
at least once a day

The jersey shore on a warm summer day full of the summer beach smells…coconut oil and cotton candy…the colors of the season are everywhere turquoise blue, sun yellow, and pink like the cheeks of children at play making sand castles…and wading pools for incoming waves, tiny treasures scattered everywhere, the taste of summer on the boardwalk sweet ice-cream melting between soft warm waffles. With the warm sun, & the giant clown peering down there is nothing left to do but smile

Dressed to the 9's
and strutting his stuff
she fell head over heels
in love
at first sight.

As he held her gently in a close embrace, she dared to breathe deeply and open her eyes…afraid of heights , and afraid to let herself trust again, she concentrated on the feeling of his strong arms around her, and listened carefully to his whispered promises, and she knew in her heart that in time, her fears would subside, and love would take control…and this time she would enjoy the ride

Her photographic memory
left little need to develop the film,
until she decided
to share
her vision

If just can't get your ducks in a row,
at the very least,
line up your smiling turtles.

Sometimes you have to take a leap of faith
and trust
that your wings will unfurl
on the way down
and only then can you soar
to heights
you never would have
imagined

When asked, "How are you?"
His reply never varied,
"Just ducky!" he would answer,
& smile as he went on his way...

Late September while most of the garden is fading,
the sunflower, having reached for the sky all summer while
filling beehives with sweet nectar.
Now, gracefully, bows her head to the earth
bearing an abundance of food
for the long winter nap...

The colors of autumn, like a rainbow at our feet. The crisp sound of leaves fills the air. The scent of impending frost is near...

A season for changes, the leaves as they change their colors, the changes our wardrobes make to keep us warm,

A season of endings and beginnings...as the gardens bear the fruits of an entire summers work, as the perennials show their last colors and turn to hide in the warm earth till next spring, as the carefree days of summer come to a close and children return to their desks and classrooms to study for another 10 months (or so)... time to start thinking just how you will manage to get through the long cold winter ahead...

The fool, with no strings attached,
fell flat on his face
with no hope of ever getting back on his feet...

This being only one of the many downsides to living the
free unattached life, he once thought so appealing. I'm
sure, eventually; someone came along, and helped
him up. Maybe changed his mind & attached at
least a few strings, to keep him on his feet.

The flowers he brought her far outlasted the relationship, which, it turns out, was an incredibly good thing! His generosity and attentiveness hid, quite cleverly, the narcissist that he truly was. On learning this undisclosed fact, she realized she could have just bought her own flowers…it would have saved a lot of confusion.

The simple beauty of a seed not yet planted,
allows our imaginations to wander
and ponder
the beauty of the thought
it will eventually inspire...

Shades of summer, shades of winter –
Flip-flops waiting for warmer weather and warmer feet!

Never really put the flip-flops away…it's nice to see them
sitting there in the coat closet, their summer colors a
bright smile against the dull colors of winters shoes and
boots…. and if by some luck of the draw we happen to get
a day mid-January were the temperature rises above 50,
you can quickly slip them on and go out to get the mail
and make believe that summer is only a step away…

Just the sight of a flip-flop keeps the faith alive that
warmer times are coming, when the sun will feel
so delicious on bare skin that I will quickly forget
how dull and long the winter months are….
I probably belong somewhere else, where summers are longer
and only an autumn or spring interferes with the joy that
summer brings. Arizona, California, a sunny island…

After the rain stopped,
the sun came out,
making diamonds out of rain drops,
drying tears from tired eyes,
and bringing with it a feeling of hope
and possibilities
she couldn't have seen
in the darkness of the storm....

Early spring day, the old metal of the chair is a bit of a
shock to newly bared legs… warming with time…
watching the leaves dance their happy dance of life,
listening to the song of the water falling from
a rain swollen lake… and the birds singing
songs of love to the newly hatched…
the turtles rusty in color from their long winters mud bath…
on an early spring day even an old heart can feel young again.

sit a while watch the tides change guard
& the sea birds glide,
just sit,
there's no need for talk
we only need listen to
our hearts.

"Get a room!" The treasure hunter bellowed as he strode past the couple, on the otherwise deserted beach. Separating for a minute to look in his direction they laughed. Watching him, silhouetted by the sun against the ocean, swinging his metal detector back and forth. The sun caressing their faces with new spring warmth and the breezes brushing hair back from their faces…

As the strange little man disappeared down the coastline alone, they turned toward each other again…to finish the interrupted kiss… and their own search for something to treasure…

Even when you think you get a peek
Inside someone else's head, there is still so much more to discover,
so many more rooms and boxes and filing cabinets where
anything could be resting…safely away…from prying eyes.

Proof that even the smallest stone,
when caught between a rock and a hard place
…in this instance–another rock…
can muster up the strength from within to stay
strong, to fight the fight, or simply keep the
rock from squashing his smaller friend…

Sitting at the edge of the land,
just watching God make waves and toss treasures
to the sand…just sitting, just watching…
it's hard to remember the small things
that had you so annoyed only hours ago…
just sitting here, feeling so small against the grandeur
of God's creations…feeling so safe, in His hands…
sitting at the edge of the land….

Mom's night out, laughing till we cry tears of insanity.
Stories told between fits of laughter,
stories of mundane things gone terribly wrong,
Holding our sides for fear they will split open.
Every breath just barely enough to keep us conscious
As the laughter subsides, someone cries breathlessly:
"Ooo, the tears are running down my leg!"
and we start laughing all over again
in the process forgetting
just what it was that got us started, but it doesn't matter,
it only matters that we laugh and that we have each other...

A great analogy came up today…scattered thoughts, when you try to make sense of one it knocks three others into action… kind of like pick up sticks—that old-fashioned game that required no batteries or electricity. Just a steady hand—and some days my thoughts can so very much be a pile of pick up sticks…I try to sort out one issue and in the process send 3 other thoughts racing for my attention and in the end nothing gets solved…so I need to line up my sticks… where I can pick up one at a time…look it over sort it out and put it back into the cylinder where it belongs… Then there are the days where the thoughts and ideas get so backed up it's more like an avalanche of thoughts barreling down on me…burying me so deep, it's all I can do to breathe…

Possibly needing more time to relax and just look at the pick up sticks?

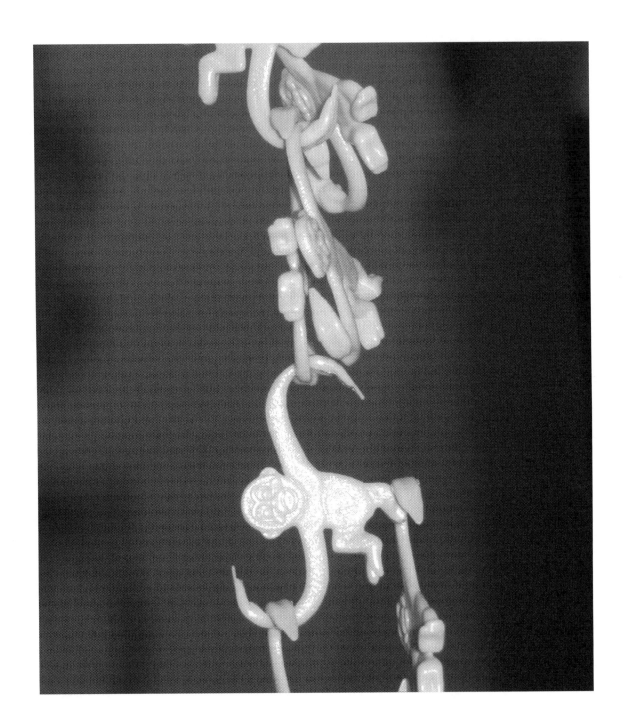

...or as a friend suggested, if you are too young and your grandma was giving you a barrel of monkeys instead... you go to pick up one thought, one monkey, and find there are two or three others hanging on for dear life, and you have to try to pay attention to all of them at once...

Here is one of those un-expected, mid-winter, flip flop days. Happily I had a pair stashed under the seat of my car. Everyone was so joyfully surprised by the sunshine filled day that they all peeled off as many layers as they possibly could and danced along the frigid ocean waves....

I told them over and over
Get in the house before the snow comes
You're not human
The first kiss of a snowflake
& You'll be turned to stone....
(Or is that cement?)
They wouldn't listen....

no flip-flops today, even the snow boots aren't high
enough to keep the snow in it's place.... however,
the snow is enough to keep us inside, warm and cozy
and listening to the beautiful silence of winter...

It's not really so much about the life lessons,
rather what you do with them.
I've known people who will never learn only because
they are never truly listening.
I sincerely believe that everything does happen for a reason,
yes we have the gift of free will, however,
I also sincerely believe that if we listen to our hearts first we
will make the choice we need to make at that moment.
Not to say that every choice is the one that leads to
happily ever after but on the path to discovering
just what constitutes happily ever after for each of us,
we have a journey to make, lessons to learn,
hearts to fill and mend when broken.
The journey is so much more enjoyable when we are fortunate
enough to be surrounded by true friends and family that love
us unconditionally, sometimes more than we love ourselves…